Hidden in the Trees

Barbara Taylor

QED Publishing

The words in **bold** are explained in the Glossary on page 22.

Front cover: A green tree snake hides among the green leaves in its rainforest home.

Project Editor: Angela Royston
Designer: Matthew Kelly
Picture Researcher: Maria Joannou

Copyright © QED Publishing 2011

First published in the UK in 2011 by
QED Publishing
A Quarto Group Company
226 City Road
London EC1V 2TT
www.qed-publishing.co.uk

ISBN 978 1 84835 604 7

Printed in China

Picture credits

(t=top, b=bottom, r=right, l=left, fc=front cover, bc=back cover)
Corbis Ocean Collection 8-9, Staffan Widstrand 9r, Tom Brakefield 12;
FLPA Thomas Marent/Minden Pictures 5b, 14, Silvestris Fotoservice 16,
Konrad Wothe/Minden Pictures 19b, G E Hyde 20; **Nature Picture Library**
Tim Laman 1, 4, Premaphotos 11t, Phil Savoie 13b; **Photolibrary** Animals
Animals/Nigel JH. Smith 10, Juniors Bildarchiv 11b, Bruno Cavignaux
15b, Imagebroker.net/GTW GTW 17, Animals Animals/Marian Bacon 21t;
Photoshot NHPA/Anthony Bannister 5r, NHPA/Cortez Austin 6, NHPA/Daniel
Heuclin 7t, NHPA/A.N.T. Photo Library 13t, 21b, NHPA/Stephen Dalton
15t, NHPA/Daniel Heuclin 18-19; **Shutterstock** worldswildlifewonders fc,
arnausd weiser bc, Szefei 2-3, Clearviewstock 7b, szefei 22-23, 24.

Contents

Hiding in the trees

Animals that live in hot, steamy **rainforests** are good at hide and seek. The animals hide by blending in with all the trees and plants around them. This is called **camouflage**.

Some animals are green to match the leaves on the trees. The colour of green pigeons hides them from hunters, especially when the pigeons keep still.

▶ Pigeons are hard to see among the green leaves. They hide as they feed on fruit growing on the trees.

Wood and dead leaves

Many animals look like twigs, bark or thorns. When leaf-tailed geckos rest on tree trunks during the day, they are almost invisible.

Piles of dry, brown leaves cover the ground beneath the trees. The patterns of some animals, such as a snake called a gaboon viper, match these dead leaves.

patterned skin

HIDE AND SEEK

A gaboon viper is hiding among these dead leaves. Can you follow its body from one end to the other?

▲ The colour and patterns on the gecko's skin blend in with the bark of the tree.

5

Hunting in the trees

Rainforests are full of food for hungry hunters. Fierce birds swoop down from the sky, while snakes coil around the tree branches.

The harpy eagle is the biggest and strongest eagle in the world. A harpy eagle is well camouflaged by its speckled grey feathers. The eagle chases monkeys and other animals in the treetops, and then catches them in its **talons**, or big claws.

strong, hooked beak for tearing meat from bones

sharp, curved talons

▲ A harpy eagle returns to its nest in the trees.

Predators and prey

Animals that hunt are called **predators**. The animals they hunt are their **prey**. Snakes, such as green tree pythons, coil themselves around a branch. They wait for their prey to come really close before they strike.

Green tree frogs feed on **insects** and so they are predators, too. As the frogs sleep during the day, their green colour hides them from birds and reptiles, such as snakes and lizards, that hunt them.

▲ A green tree python hangs from a branch.

big eyes for seeing at night

wide mouth for catching insects

long, thin toes for gripping branches

ANIMAL TALK

- Tree snakes have ridges on their belly to help them grip onto the branches.

- Tree frogs have large, sticky **suckers** under their toes.

7

Jungle cats

A jaguar's spots hide it among the shadows and patches of sunlight shining through the trees. A tiger's stripes camouflage it, too.

Jaguars hunt for wild pigs, deer and other animals. These big cats cannot run as fast as their prey. Their camouflage helps them to get very close to their prey before they are seen.

Black panthers

Sometimes, jaguars are born with black fur. These black jaguars are called black panthers. They are very hard to see among the dark shadows and at night-time.

▶ A jaguar creeps along a low branch. It is ready to leap onto any prey that passes by below.

ears for hearing the smallest sounds

black marks inside a ring of black spots

▶ Tigers are the biggest cats in the world.

CAT FACTS

- Jaguars and tigers never meet in the wild. Tigers come from Asia but jaguars come from Central and South America.

- A tiger sharpens and cleans its claws by scraping them on trees.

- Every jaguar's fur has a different pattern of black spots.

Hiding from hunters

Many different animals are hunted by jungle predators. Hunted animals include lizards and monkeys in the trees, and pigs and agoutis on the ground.

Camouflage helps hunted animals to stay alive. The speckled brown fur of agoutis blends with the brown shadows under the trees. These shy animals also avoid predators by hiding in their **burrows**.

very sharp, strong teeth

five fingers for holding food

▲ An agouti blends in with the light and dark shadows on the ground.

Clever tricks

A flying lizard escapes from predators by gliding between the trees. It opens two wings made of thin skin. Its body is the same colour as the tree bark. So when the lizard folds its wings it disappears!

▲ A flying lizard is sometimes called a flying dragon.

big ears to listen for predators

big eyes for seeing in shady places

Okapis sometimes escape from hungry predators by standing still! An okapi's stripes make it difficult for a predator to see the shape of the whole animal.

ANIMAL TALK

- Agoutis are the only animals, apart from parrots, that can crack open Brazil nuts.

- An okapi can use its long tongue to clean its eyes!

11

Babies and chicks

Rainforests have plenty of places for babies and chicks to hide. Even so, they are in constant danger because they are so small and weak. They cannot fight predators or run away fast, so they hide instead!

Baby animals are often better camouflaged than their parents. Adult tapirs are plain brown, but young tapirs have spots and stripes. They are hard to see in the patchy light on the brown forest floor.

▲ A young tapir loses its spots and stripes when it is about one year old.

A striped cassowary chick blends in with the dead leaves on the ground.

Dull colours

Male birds, such as birds of paradise, are often brightly coloured to attract females. But the females usually have dull colours to hide them while they sit on their eggs.

The chicks of forest birds are well camouflaged too. They either have dull colours or they have spots or stripes, like cassowary chicks.

female

male

A male bird of paradise dances along a branch to show off his colourful feathers to a female.

ANIMAL TALK

- Male birds of paradise can dance for hours.

- Tapirs are good swimmers and often jump into rivers to avoid jaguars.

13

Clever disguises

Lots of animals eat insects in the rainforest, so insects have to be very good at hiding from predators. Some insects **disguise** themselves as plants.

spikes on front legs for holding prey

sharp jaws

Flaps on the legs of the flower mantis look like flower petals. These fierce insects sit on flowers and wait for an insect to fly past. Then they quickly grab it.

▲ **This flower mantis is hanging upside down so that it looks like part of the flower.**

Dead leaves

Dead leaves make a good disguise because animals don't want to eat them. When a leaf butterfly closes its wings, it looks just like a dead leaf.

The matamata turtle's bumpy shell looks like dead leaves, too. The turtle hides underwater in muddy rivers. When a fish swims past, the turtle opens its big mouth and sucks the fish inside, like a vacuum cleaner.

HIDE AND SEEK

The tails on the back wings of a leaf butterfly look like leaf stalks. Can you spot the leaf butterfly hiding among these dead leaves?

long, wide neck

rough, bumpy shell

very small eyes

▲ A matamata turtle waits on the bottom of a rainforest river.

Changing colour

Some rainforest animals change colour to make their camouflage better. Chameleons can change as they move from one background to another, but sloths hardly move at all!

Sloths have grey-brown fur, which helps to hide them as they hang from branches high in the trees. In the **rainy season**, tiny plants grow on their damp hair. Then their fur looks green, like the fresh green leaves growing around them.

◄ A sloth's fur grows down from its stomach to its back, so the rain runs off when it hangs upside down.

Chameleon camouflage

Chameleons can change colour quite quickly. Their colour changes as the day gets brighter and hotter, and as the evening becomes darker and cooler.

Some chameleons change colour to match their background. Patches of colour move in the skin, or become bigger or smaller.

◄ This chameleon has just caught an insect on the end of its long tongue.

long, sticky tongue

ANIMAL TALK

- Sloths spend 20 hours a day snoozing in trees.

- Most chameleons live only on the African island of Madagascar.

Living sticks

When stick insects keep very still, they look just like the twigs or leaves of rainforest plants. Stick insects even move their legs to match the way the plants sway in the breeze.

▶ This stick insect looks like the leaves around it.

Giant stick insects live in rainforests in Indonesia in South East Asia. They are the longest insects in the world, yet they are so well camouflaged they merge into the forest.

Legging it

Young stick insects hang from twigs. If they are disturbed, they fall off the twigs, just like dead leaves falling down to the ground.

Stick insects can actually break off their legs to escape from a predator. Don't worry! The legs soon grow back again.

▶ Stick insects are hard to tell apart from the twigs of plants they live on.

INSECT FACTS

- Stick insects hold their legs at the same angle as the twigs around them.

- A giant stick insect can be as long as your arm!

19

Tricks and poisons

Some rainforest animals do not need camouflage because they are protected in other ways. Some scare predators away by pretending to be big, dangerous animals. Other animals contain nasty **poisons.**

Owl moths do not need to hide, because the coloured markings on their wings look like an owl's big eyes and feathers. Birds are frightened of owls, so they avoid these big moths.

false eye

feathery patterns

▲ The owl moth lives in rainforests in India and eastern Asia.

Beware — poison!

Tiny poison arrow frogs do not mind if predators see them. Their bright colours are a warning that means: "Don't eat me! I taste nasty."

Birdwing butterfly caterpillars take in poisons from the plants they eat. Their bright colours also warn birds not to eat them.

▼ A poison arrow frog makes some poison in its skin, but it also takes in poisons from poisonous insects and other food.

- A few drops of poison from a poison arrow frog are strong enough to kill a horse.

- An owl moth's wingspan is up to 16 centimetres. That's as big as a small bird!

⊲······ damp skin

◄ The caterpillar of a birdwing butterfly has colourful spines on its back. The spines are filled with poison!

long back legs for leaping

Glossary

burrow A long tunnel dug in the soil by animals such as agoutis.

camouflage Colours, patterns or markings that help an animal to hide by matching their background.

disguise When an animal makes itself look like another animal or a plant.

insect An animal with six legs and three parts to its body. Butterflies and flower mantises are insects.

poison A chemical substance that kills or injures living things.

predator An animal that hunts and kills other animals for food.

prey An animal that is hunted and killed by a predator.

rainforest A forest that grows in places near the Equator, where it is hot and wet all year round. It is sometimes called a jungle.

rainy season The time of year when it rains hard every day.

suckers Round pads on parts of the body that can hold tightly to something, such as a tree.

talon A curved claw on the foot of a bird of prey. Talons are long, thick and very sharp.

Did you spot them?
The head of the gaboon viper hiding on page 5 is near the bottom of the photo and its tail is at the top. The leaf butterfly on page 15 is in the middle of the photo. Maybe you can see its feelers on the right first?

Index

Notes for parents and teachers

As you share this book with children, ask questions to encourage them to look closely at the detail in the photographs.

More about trees

- Trees are large, tall plants with a woody main stem, or trunk, and a spreading crown of branches high above the ground.
- Tree roots help to support the tree as well as the ground around it. Explain to children that roots bind the soil together. When people destroy forests, soil is washed away by the rain.
- Bark stops the trees from drying out and protects them. Ask children to find different types of bark near them (rough, smooth, lined, peeling) and make bark rubbing patterns with thick crayons.
- Leaves make food for the tree, and veins in the leaves transport the food to the rest of the tree. The children could paint leaves and press them onto paper to make leaf prints.
- Rainforest trees are usually 30 to 50 metres tall and live for a long time. They usually have green leaves on their branches all year long, but they also lose some leaves all year round. This is why the forest floor is covered in a carpet of dead leaves.
- Ask the children to make a collage of a huge rainforest tree using the different techniques above.

Rainforests

- Rainforests have an annual rainfall of 250 centimetres and temperatures between 23 and 31 degrees Celsius all year round.
- Try to plan an outing to a zoo or wildlife park that has a rainforest enclosure so the children can get a better idea of the heat and moisture that shape these environments.

Moving around

- Camouflage works best when animals keep still, but sometimes they have to move to find food or escape from predators!
- Sticky toes, rough scales or long claws give rainforest animals extra gripping power on wet, slippery surfaces. This is why it is important for children not to run next to a swimming pool – their feet are so slippery they could fall!

Hunters and hunted

- Rainforest insects are especially well camouflaged because they are a major source of food for hungry hunters.
- There is so much food available in rainforests all year round that some animals can grow to giant sizes. Explain to the children that an anaconda can be several times as long as they are!